Exploring a Theme Sacred Stories

'The great religious stories, those that have stood the test of time and crossed cultural divides, are made universally relevant by their capacity to be constantly reinterpreted and endlessly renewed.'

Sacred texts are often story texts. Use of creative and imaginative storytelling and follow-up activities not only helps children to hear and learn about traditional, timeless faith stories valued within religions and central to sacred texts, it also gives children a glimpse 'inside' these stories – of the 'spiritual heart' at the centre. Children need to be given opportunities to engage with such stories at their own levels and to respond to them in their own ways, finding their own meanings.

This publication suggests some ways of engaging children with faith stories and sacred text. Wherever possible we have asked people from within faith communities to tell us which stories and texts they would use with children, why and how. Faith always uses story to explore truths in life and to impact on life – education needs the same.

Are you telling enough? Are your pupils creatively engaged in responding? Could you plan some exciting new approaches? This publication will give you a few new starting points.

For further ideas see *Developing Primary RE: Faith Stories* (ISBN 978-1-904024-23-1) and *Developing Primary RE: Stories about God* (ISBN 978-1-904024-68-2), both available from RE Today.

Joyce Mackley
Editor

RE Today weblink:
www.retoday.org.uk

The RE Today website provides some free additional resources and classroom ready materials for subscribers. Look out for the 'RE Today on the web' logo at the end of selected articles.

The password for access can be found in each term's *REtoday* magazine.

'Our books are special!'

For the teacher

Special books is a key theme in many RE syllabuses. A typical focus question for planning in the 4–7 age group might be *Why are holy books special?*

Such a unit is likely to focus on helping children know something about the holy books of Christianity and one other religion – who uses them, how they are used, why they are important and what they contain. But perhaps the most important learning we would want to take place during these activities would be for children to begin to recognise just how much these 'special' books matter to believers – that, for many, these books are in fact 'holy' or 'sacred'.

The activities on the following two pages focus on helping 5–7 year olds think about how Christians, Jews and Muslims treat their special books (how they are carried, touched, opened, stored) in unusual ways, and what this tells us. Activities could be applied to other religions such as Sikhism. Part of the process will be to get children thinking about how they treat the things that are really special to them, and to begin to recognise that there is a difference between 'special' and 'sacred'.

Learning outcomes

So that they can

- **give examples** of books and stories which are very special to people and **say why**
- **talk about some of the ways** believers treat their special books which show us how special they are
- **talk about the meaning of some special books and stories for believers** *making connections with their own lives.*

Classroom starter activities

- **Teacher brings in a book which has special significance for her/ him** (for example a wedding photo album) and talks about why it is special to her/him and how s/he would like it to be treated.

- **Paired talk:** Do you have a book as special as the teacher's special book? What is it? Why is it so special? How would you feel if it was damaged?

- **Listen** to children's ideas about how we should handle and look after something that is very important and special to someone. Role-play showing someone a really important book.

- **Have a display of books.** This will include special books that the teacher and the children have brought in, some versions of the Bible, a Qur'an which is on its stand and covered, placed higher than other books, and a replica Torah scroll in its cover. Take a photograph of the display and enlarge for display purposes.

- Ask pupils to look at the books and select two books they would like to **ask questions** about. These questions can be put on card and attached to the photo of the display.

- Some questions should be dealt with quickly, but more time and focus needs to be given to questions about the **Bible**, the **Qur'an** and the **Torah** scroll: such questions as 'Why is this book important and special?' 'Who wrote this book?' and 'What is this book about?' 'Why is this book on a stand?' 'Why is the scroll covered?

RE Today weblink:

www.retoday.org.uk

Subscribers can download page 4 for use in the classroom, and an Early Years Foundation Stage unit planner on 'Our books are special', from the RE Today website www.retoday.org.uk (go to REtoday Curriculum Books web supplement).

The Bible – a holy book

- **Visit a church or chapel**. Before the visit, discuss where you might find the Bible, if it is very important to Christians and an important part of worship. **Challenge the children to find the Bible** (often on an ornate lectern, in a prominent position at the front). **Talk about:** What does this suggest about how Christians feel about their holy book?

- Explain that the Bible is full of stories, poems and wise sayings. **Invite a Christian from the school community to come and talk to the children about why the Bible is special and holy for them. Ask them to tell or read a favourite story from the Bible,** and to explain to the children why they like it so much.

- If appropriate, **children could act out the story**, and **talk about** the reasons why it was important to the visitor.

- Extend children's learning by **viewing and talking about** a brief DVD/web clip suitable for 5–7s such as the opening couple of minutes of *What is the Bible?* on the BBC Learning Zone (www.bbc.co.uk/learningzone/clips).

The Jewish Torah – a holy book

- **Look at DVD/web clips** to show a Torah scroll in use, for example BBC Learning Zone Clips for the classroom: 'The Synagogue' (navigate to the primary RE section) (www.bbc.co.uk/learningzone/clips). Watch a three-minute clip. **Ask children to 'be detectives' – what do they notice** about the 'special book'? **Paired talk:** What clues did they spot? How do they know that the Torah is very important? (e.g. kept in a special cupboard (The Ark) covered, carried carefully, very big! not touched (use of Yad).

- Explain that Jews believe that the Torah is God's way of communicating with them. It is his most precious gift to them.

- **Either use the activity on page 4 or display line drawings of Yad, Ark, Bimah, Mantle** (cover for Torah) on the whiteboard (or on paper) and ask children to complete the sentence 'We know that the Torah is a very special book because . . .'.

The Muslim Qur'an – a holy book

- Without telling children what it is, bring a wrapped copy of the Qur'an into the classroom, together with a folded Qur'an stand. Spread a cloth out on a table and place both down carefully.

- Make a big display of washing your hands before carefully unwrapping the book and placing it on the opened Qur'an stand.

- Ask children to talk about what these actions show them about the book.

- Invite children in small groups to look closely at the book, tell others what they notice, and suggest some questions they would like to **ask**.

- Explain that Muslims believe that the words found in the Qur'an came from God, that they were revealed to Muhammad by the Angel Jibril (Gabriel). Watch a clip to hear the story of Muhammad in the cave: www.bbc.co.uk/learningzone/clips. Who was Muhammad?

- Decide together how they can best look after this special book whilst it is in the classroom – for example where it should be kept (high up).

DRAW THE MISSING PICTURE

The pictures around this page show some of the ways one holy book is treated.

Fill in the writing bubbles and draw a picture in the space below to show which book you think this is

This cupboard is called ......

What is kept inside it?

This is called a ...

It is used for....

What is this lady holding?

What can you see on top?

This special desk is called a ....

It is used for.......

My picture shows

Word List: YAD   BIMAH   ARK   SCROLLS   TORAH

Using sacred story with young children

For the teacher

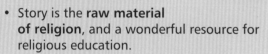

Story touches parts other words don't reach!

- Story is the **raw material of religion**, and a wonderful resource for religious education.

- Used effectively, story **can open the door to a world way beyond** the child's own. If we make the most of its potential, its resonance with children's own lives will be illuminating.

- Story is **unmatched in its potential to promote children's learning**, both about and from religion.

The following pages identify some principles to help you make the most of faith stories with very young children, and illustrate these by taking you through the approach applied to the Hindu story of how Ganesha got his elephant head.

Expectations and outcomes

Early Learning Foundation Stage
The activities outlined here make a particular contribution to the development of:

- communication, language and literacy: attentive listening, describing, using vocabulary

- knowledge and understanding of the world: awareness of different beliefs and cultures.

5–7 year olds:
As a result of these activities children should be able to:

- talk about how Ganesha came to have an elephant's head and which animal head they would choose for themselves and why. (Level 1)

- thoughtfully retell the story of Ganesha, using the correct names, and talk about a time when, like Shiva, they were really sorry for something they had done. (Level 2)

Key principles for using sacred story in the classroom

- Choose a story that grabs you and be prepared to wonder at it. Use the most **authentic** version of the story available to you.

- **Know** what the story is about! Noah, for example, is often chosen because it is thought of as a 'nice little story'. Many teachers simply do not appreciate that the biblical myth is really all about divine retribution and God's covenant.

- Learn the story well enough to **tell it rather than read it**, and **keep eye contact** with listeners.

- **Create an atmosphere** which sets this time apart.

- **Engage children's whole brain** (use music, tactile stimuli, fantasy exercises).

- **Invite children to 'come into' the story**, live it and become intimate with it, always ensuring you safeguard children's integrity and that of their families.

- **Think about timing** and the drama of the narrative; **use pauses for effect** in your telling.

- **Identify questions** that probe the story and highlight issues of importance to the children rather than simply prompt recall of the story details.

- **Don't be afraid of silence** when you invite children's responses, as long as they are thinking.

- **Enjoy** having your listeners 'in the palm of your hand'!

See also

These activities are from the **Gift to the Child** approach to teaching and learning in RE with younger children. For further story and activity details see: M Grimmett, J Grove, J Hull and L Tellam, *A Gift to the Child* (original) and Series Two (2006) Articles of Faith ISBN 978-1-874630-15-9.

Teachers TV: Storytelling workshop: KS1/2 RE http://www.teachers.tv/video/3067

Some practical ways of marking out time and space for a 'faith story' in the classroom

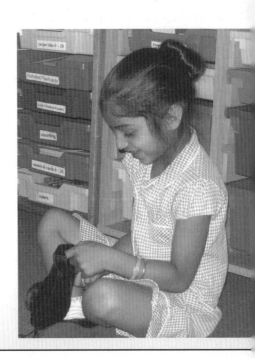

Engaging young learners with faith stories

A sacred story can be introduced in a variety of ways to capture children's interest and to help listeners 'find' the story. For example:

* A mysterious object, concealed in black velvet or in a 'mystery bag', becomes the focus for some speculation and is slowly and deliberately disclosed. For example: a rosary before the story of St Bernadette.

* A sound: for example the sound of the Adhan brings children into the story of the Bilal and the first Call to Prayer; nails hammered into a piece of wood signal a powerful invitation into the Easter story.

Through this engagement children begin to develop a relationship with the story.

Marking out faith stories

Sacred stories are treasures from the heart of a religious tradition which, for some people, are holy ground.

They can only be accessed in one of two ways:

* through faith: handed down to children by their parents and their faith community

* through the imagination: the school route.

In the classroom children need to be invited to get close to the sacred but also be safeguarded from it. There can be no assumptions about belief or commitment on the part of children.

An effective strategy for 'marking out' faith stories is through the use of 'entering devices'. An 'entering device' is an action that says 'come in' at the start of the story, and repeated at the close., signals the end of the 'faith' story for children. This 'device' marks out the leaving of the 'religious world' and protects the child from stepping over the threshold into faith.

Come into a faith story through:

	Lighting the story candle
	Ringing the story bell
	Striking the singing bowl
	Spreading out a coloured cloth placing an artefact in the centre
	Playing music

The story of Ganesha

[Light the story candle]

Ganesha is standing guard outside his mother's door. She is Parvati, a goddess, and he knows she mustn't be disturbed in her bath. He's very proud to be trusted with this job and he wants to do it well.

Suddenly in the quietness he hears a tremendous noise like a huge rushing wind coming from a long way away. He finds it hard to stand up. There in front of him is the mighty figure of the great god Shiva. His voice booms like thunder as he comes towards the door . . .

Ganesha can't let him go in, he mustn't, but what can he do? He stretches and holds his head up high, although his tummy feels like jelly. 'You can't go in there,' he says in the biggest voice he can find. 'Parvati is not to be disturbed and it's my job to protect her.'

Shiva is furious. Parvati is his wife and no one will tell him where he cannot go. Fiercely, he draws out a sharp knife and cuts off the little boy's head. Oh! . . . Ganesha is dead.

Parvati hears the commotion and comes to find out what is happening. When she sees her beloved little boy dead at Shiva's feet, she breaks her heart. Between her sobs, she tells her husband that she was lonely so she made a child from flakes of her skin and breathed life into him. How could he kill him? Of course, when he knows about Ganesha, Shiva is sorry. He will do anything to make Parvati smile again. So he sets off to find a new head for the little boy.

It so happens that the first creature Shiva meets is an elephant. What a wonderful head that would be for Ganesha, he thinks. Shiva carries the elephant's head back to Parvati and sets it onto the child's body. There! Parvati is thrilled to have her little boy back; she cuddles him and laughs when he looks up at her with his big dark eyes and wraps his new trunk round her neck. She loves his big ears too! She is delighted that now her son has been made by Shiva as well as by her. And Ganesha finds that he can do all sorts of things with his new head that he couldn't do with the old one!

[Extinguish the candle]

Seat children comfortably on the carpet. Have a figure of Ganesha hidden inside a mystery bag and a candle ready for lighting. Be familiar with the story (see page 7).

Explain to children that they are going to hear an important story, one which is 'holy' or 'sacred' for some people. To show this, a candle will be lit whilst the story is told.

Teaching strategy

**ENGAGEMENT
Introduction to Ganesha through the child's imagination**

Imagine a little boy with four arms, a fat belly and an elephant head.

What does an elephant's head look like?

Can you see his big ears, long trunk and curved tusks?

**ENTERING DEVICE
Candle**

Light the story candle

**DISCOVERY
Story of Ganesha's birth
Unveiling the figure of Ganesha**

- Tell the story
- Extinguish the candle
- Ask reflective questions
- Slowly and deliberately disclose the shrine figure of Ganesha
- Invite children to talk about what they can see and what they are thinking.

**DISTANCING DEVICE
A Hindu child who worships Ganesha
(Placing the story in the faith context)**

Show children posters of a Ganesha murti in a home shrine or Hindu temple today.

Explain that for some people Ganesha is God and they worship him. Show how a Hindu child worships Ganesha. Hindu worship is called *puja*.

**REFLECTION
Linking to children's own experience**

Some questions you might ask

- What did you think about the story? What was frightening about it?
- If you had a new (animal) head, what would you like it to be?
- When, like Ganesha, have you been given something important to do? How does it feel?
- When have you been really sorry for something you've done? How did you put it right?

Favourite stories from sacred books: activities to get children speaking and listening

For the teacher

Faith stories and storytelling is at the heart of all religious traditions. Encouraging those for whom particular stories have the greatest meaning to share these with children, in an open and educationally appropriate way, is at the heart of the activities outlined here.

The process

We asked each faith visitor to:

- identify a favourite story from their sacred book to tell children during their visit – and identify some objects or artefacts to bring along to interest and engage children with the story and its meaning.

- tell the children about why they chose this particular story; talk about what it means for them, and help children to think about an important message in the story which might be relevant to everyone.

- talk about how and why the Bible/Torah /Qur'an (as appropriate to the visitor) is a very special sacred book, how they use it and why it is so important for them personally.

This approach can be used with your own visitors from any faith community. We have suggested some follow-up activities to help children talk about and respond to the story and sacred book. You will be able to suggest others linked to the literacy framework for speaking and listening.

Expectations and outcomes

The following pupil-friendly criteria could be used to assess children's responses. Level 2 describes what most 7-year-olds should be able to do.

I can...

1 I can...	• **use some religious words to talk about** a story that is special to a visitor; say why the visitor liked this story; **talk about some feelings connected with the story** and times I may have felt like this.
2 I can...	• **use some religious words to retell** a favourite story of a faith visitor, name the holy book the story came from and **talk about why** the story is important for the visitor. • **talk about and express in writing pictures something in my own experience that the story made me think about.**

See also

Two short digital video clips suitable for 5–7s to illustrate how worshippers show great respect towards their sacred books:

- Torah scroll in use in the synagogue, St Anne's, Lancashire http://www.cleo.net.uk/resources/index.php?ks=2&cur=15

- Sikh morning ceremony focused on the Guru Granth Sahib http://www.cleo.net.uk/resources/index.php?ks=2&cur=15

For the teacher

Salma

Meet Salma

'Hello, my name is Salma. I am a Muslim who was born and brought up in London but now I live in Gloucester. I am also a mother, wife, sister, daughter, niece. I work in an infant school. I don't have my own class, but I am lucky enough to work with all Reception, Year 1 and Year 2 classes. My main language is English, but I am also able to read key phrases in Arabic, Urdu and Gujarati.

My daughter is 10 and likes 'spag bol' and lasagne; and watching the Disney channel! As a family we are quite sporty. I enjoy netball, basketball, cycling, aerobics and body combat exercises. My daughter also enjoys netball, cross country running, cycling and, like my husband, football and swimming. We support Tottenham Football Club, and England. We have all been to England matches at Old Trafford and Wembley.

A story from Islam I really like is the story of Abraham (Ibrahim) and the tests (sacrifices) he is asked to make by God. I like to use 'The Great Sacrifice' in *My First Qur'an* by Saniyasnain Khan to help me retell this story for children (see page 11).

This story is very special for me because it reminds me of Id ul Adha, a special festival that Muslims celebrate, and of the journey (the Hajj) that all Muslims must make to Makkah to re-enact the story that happened over 4000 years ago. And also of a special promise that God made to Abraham, that he (God) would never test mankind like this again.

The Muslim holy book, the Qur'an, is such a special book to me because not only does its contents guide me; shows me the correct way of life; has lots of prayers; charts the history of mankind and the lives of so many great Prophets, their wives, mothers, daughters and sisters; it is a source of inspiration for me and the Muslim Ummah (community) to model our lives on such great people such as Jesus, Mary, Job, and so on.

Activities

When telling children the story of 'The Great Sacrifice' from the Qur'an, Salma suggests:

- **Acting out** parts of the story and getting children to help.

- **Asking children to talk about** how Ismail might have felt when his father told him about his dream (might he have been worried, frightened?) Why was he *not* afraid? How did Ismail and Ibrahim feel when the angel Jibril appeared with the ram? Ask children to act out someone feeling really happy. Why do they think Allah sent the dream in the first place? (If children have understood the story they will say it was a test for Abraham to find out if he trusted Allah!)

- **Talk about why the Qur'an is such a special book for Salma.** Look at a Qur'an together. Role-play and talk about how Salma would handle it and what these actions show about the meaning of this 'sacred' book for believers

- **With a partner, work out a good question to ask** Salma (or their own Muslim visitor) about her favourite story or the Qur'an as a special book for her. Share these questions. Ask and receive some answers – try emailing the visitor

Muslim story resource sheet

THE GREAT SACRIFICE

One night the Prophet Ibrahim had a dream. He was ordered by Allah to sacrifice his son. Allah talks to the prophets. But he does not talk as we talk. When he wants prophets to do something, he shows it to them in a dream.

The next day, the Prophet Ibrahim called Ismail. He said: 'Ismail, I had a dream last night. Allah wants me to sacrifice you.' Ismail was not afraid. He loved Allah very much. He knew that Allah was good and that he never does anything to harm people.

The prophet Ibrahim and Ismail left Makkah where they lived. They went to the valley of Mina. This was the place the prophet Ibrahim saw in his dream.

Ismail lay on the ground. He closed his eyes. His father stood next to him. He picked up the knife. He was ready to sacrifice his son!

At that moment the angel Jibril appeared. Allah sent the angel with a ram to be sacrificed instead. Little Ismail was saved. Ibrahim and Ismail cried with joy. They thanked Allah and then the prophet sacrificed the ram.

Ibrahim understood that Allah had been testing him to see if he would be obedient and faithful. He had passed the test!

Allah was so pleased that the prophet Ibrahim listened to him and trusted him that he commanded believers to observe this day as Id ul Adha or the festival of sacrifice.

> Based on the story from the Quran (Surah 37:102-111) as retold
> by Saniyasnain Khan in *My First Quran*, used with permission.

Things to note

This story is also found in the Jewish scriptures/Christian Old Testament (Genesis 22) with one important difference. In the Judeo/Christian story God asks Abraham to sacrifice his other son Isaac, his son with Sarah. Isma'il is his son with Hagar.

Source: My First Qur'an by Saniyasnain Khan (ISBN 8178985543) published by Goodword Books [info@goodwordbooks.com], hardback A5 size book, £6.99, available from IPCI: Islamic Vision, 434 Coventry Road, Small Heath, Birmingham B10 OJS.

email: info@islamicvision.co.uk

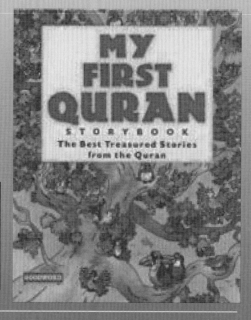

For the teacher

Meet Jane

'**Hello, my name is Jane.** I am Jewish. I was born and brought up in London in a progressive Jewish family. In my teens I went to an orthodox Jewish boarding school so I have experienced many different sides of my faith.

I have a Jewish husband and two boys Jonah and Toby who are 7 and 9. We celebrate Jewish festivals and enjoy Jewish songs and dances from all over the world. I love writing songs, which I test out with my family! The boys love singing too! I am the Town Crier for my town. The boys often come with me to events. As a family we love camping, travelling and going to music festivals.

A story from Judaism I really like is the Passover Story: in Hebrew it is called Pesach. Every year we have a special meal called the Seder meal when we celebrate this story, the story of Moses, and how he led the Jewish people out of slavery in Egypt to a new life in Israel.

The Passover story is very special for me because its message is about setting people free. Passover is a great time to think about and resolve to help people who are 'not free', who are unfairly treated and oppressed. It is also a time to try to free myself of some of the things I might otherwise become 'a slave to' – such as my own greed, desires and emotions!

The story of the Passover is written down in the Jewish holy book, the Torah. The Torah is such a special book to me because it is the guide book for my daily life. It contains 613 rules which enable Jewish people to respect God, our families and other communities. It is an important part of our tradition, with the weekly readings of the Torah in the synagogue and the rituals and customs that surround this.

Jane

Activities

When telling children the story of The Passover and the Exodus with young children Jane suggests:

- **Acting out** parts of the story and getting children to help.

- **Use a variety of props to bring the story alive:** 'a special hat for each main character; puppets for each of the plagues to make them less scary; a big piece of red netting or material for the Red Sea. You could even have characters playing the burning bush and Moses' miraculous staff.'

- **Use songs to make it lively and exciting** A good Jewish publisher is Kar-Ben Copies (or try *Two Candles Burn* by Stephen Melzack – CD available from the RE Today catalogue).

- **Follow up** by hearing about how a family today celebrates this story in spring each year at the annual Passover festival (Pesach). Take them on an imaginary visit to a Jewish person's home and role-play a Seder meal. 'Lead children to the dinner table in a circle dance, sit down and have a Seder meal together using artefacts, lighting candles, saying blessings, eating matzot (unleavened bread) and singing songs. A Seder plate for symbolic foods is the focal point.'

Jewish story resource sheet

THE PASSOVER STORY

For many years the Jewish people had been slaves ruled over by the Pharaoh of Egypt. They were working hard building pyramids and temples and were treated cruelly. The Pharaoh issued an order that all the newborn sons should be killed. A son was born to a woman called Yocheved. She wanted to save him so asked her daughter Miriam to put him in a basket amongst the reed in the River Nile. The basket was found by the Pharaoh's daughter who took the baby back to the palace and adopted him as her own son. She called him Moses. His mother was employed as a nursemaid at the palace.

As he grew up, Moses saw how the Jewish people suffered, and one day he killed a man he saw beating a slave. He ran away from the palace and went to live in Midian where he had his own family. One day whilst walking in the desert he came across a bush that was burning but did not turn to ash. It told Moses it was God and that Moses should go and ask Pharaoh to free the Jewish people from slavery. God proved to Moses that it really was Him by turning a staff into a snake, and then back again.

The Pharaoh would not let the Jewish people leave Egypt and God sent down plagues to try and encourage him to do so. These included a plague of frogs, turning the water to blood, hailstones and wild animals. Under the threat of each plague the Pharaoh said the Jewish people could leave, but when the plague had gone he would change his mind.

Moses told Pharaoh that if he did not let the people free a tenth plague would be brought on the Egyptians and all the first born Egyptians would be killed. The Jewish people were told to put a cross of lamb's blood on their doors to save their first born. The angel of death came and the Pharaoh's own son was killed amongst many others. The Pharaoh now let the Jewish people free and they quickly packed up a few belongings and fled before the Pharaoh could change his mind. They were in such a hurry that they did not have time to let their bread rise so took unleavened bread with them on their journey.

Moses led the Jewish people out of Egypt. When they reached the Red Sea, Moses touched the sea with his staff and a great miracle happened. The sea parted and the Jews passed through the pathway in the sea and escaped to freedom.

Based on the story in the book of Exodus found in the second book of the Hebrew Torah.

Niki and Andy

Meet Andy and Niki

Hello, my name is Andy. I am a Christian. I live in a town called Ludlow and although I am not a teacher I sometimes visit schools to talk about what it is like to be a follower of Jesus.

I am married to Niki, who is a teacher, and we have two children, Beth and Josh, who are both at university. I lived in Thailand when I was a boy and sometimes go back with groups to work in schools in Thailand. I love watching rugby and basketball (especially when my son Josh is playing) and like reading and watching sci-fi. We both like cooking and eating curries.

A story about Jesus I really like is the story Jesus told to explain who our neighbour is. Jesus was once asked what was the most important commandment, and his answer was: 'Love God with all your heart and love your neighbour as yourself.' Someone asked him 'Who is my neighbour?' Jesus told this story to answer the question; we sometimes call it the story of the Good Samaritan.

This story is very special for me because it helps us understand that how we treat each other is really important and that we should love and care for people even if they are different from us.

The Christian holy book, the Bible, is such a special book to me because it is full of exciting stories, history, poems, letters and advice. I have learned a lot of new things about how to enjoy being a human being from reading the Bible. It reminds me of how much God loves people and because many of the stories happened to ordinary people like you and me who made a difference, it inspires me to think about how I can make a difference. I am also excited by the fact that I have a lot to learn from the Bible still and that I often find new things when I read stories from it that I know well. It sometimes seems like a living book.

Activities

- **The Two Commandments**

Tell the children that Jesus gave his followers two guides for living:

1. To love God with all your heart, all your mind and all your strength.

2. To love your neighbour as you love yourself.

Repeat these phrases, showing actions for each word as they are spoken. Invite a child to say the commands or do the actions.

- **Tell the story of the Good Samaritan.** Ask children to improvise the story as you read; to answer the questions 'Who is my neighbour?' Who in this room is a neighbour? Who else in our lives is a neighbour? How can we love them? (If children are sitting in a circle they could take it in turns to complete the statement – 'I could love …. by ….' for another child in the class.)

- **Gifts** Put names of all the children in a hat. Each child pulls one name out and makes a card, picture, 'present' for that person, as a way of saying 'you are my neighbour'. Children could have free choice of any craft materials, but should be encouraged to think of the person they are making the 'gift' for.

- **Present gifts** – seat children back in a circle and choose a child to begin the exchange of 'gifts'. Each child who receives can then go on to give their gift away, until each child has given and received something as a way of expressing love to a neighbour.

Christian story resource sheet

THE PARABLE OF THE GOOD SAMARITAN

Jesus loved talking to people. He loved telling them about God and how God wanted people to be kind and to 'love one another'. He really wanted them to understand this – and so he told them the best way was to 'love your neighbour as you love yourself'.

One man wasn't very sure what Jesus meant by this, so he asked him a question. 'Who is my neighbour?' he asked.

Jesus answered by telling a story.

'There was once a man travelling from Jerusalem to Jericho. It was a long hot dusty road. On the way he was attacked by robbers. They took his clothes, beat him up, and went off leaving him half-dead.

Luckily, a holy man – a priest – was on his way down the same road, but when he saw him he turned away and walked on by on the other side.

Then another man came along. This man was also a holy man. He worked in the temple in Jerusalem. But he too carried on walking, taking no notice of the injured man.

Next, a visitor from another country (a Samaritan) travelling the road came across the injured man. When he saw him, his heart went out to him. He gave him first aid, disinfecting and bandaging his wounds. Then he lifted him onto his donkey, led him to an inn, and made him comfortable.

In the morning he took out two silver coins and gave them to the innkeeper, saying, "Take good care of him. If it costs any more, put it on my bill – I'll pay you on my way back."

What do you think?' Jesus asked. 'Which of the three was a neighbour to the man attacked by robbers?'

'The one who treated him kindly,' the man replied. Jesus said, 'Go and do the same.'

Based on Luke Chapter 10, verses 25–37

Things to note

At the time Jesus told this story, Jews and Samaritans were enemies. The Jewish people listening to Jesus would be very surprised to hear that it was the Samaritan who was so kind to the man who was hurt. It was not how they would expect the story to end.

See also

An excellent version for young children can be found in the *Lion Storyteller Bible* by Bob Hartman and Susie Poole, published by Lion Hudson plc (1995).

Using stories the Jewish way: a strategy for exploring sacred stories in the classroom

For the teacher

In this section Laurie Rosenberg, former headteacher of Simon Marks Jewish Primary School, Hackney, shows how a Jewish technique for exploring sacred story text can engage children, open up hidden depths and stimulate deeper application and creativity.

Pardes
Laurie's approach uses the Jewish technique of **pardes**, asking the pupils to look at the story from four dimensions.

P'shat: The literal meaning. **What does the text say** at the simplest level?

Remez: Interpretation. What does the text hint at? **What does it mean?**

D'rash: This is the Hebrew word for story and legend. **How would you tell someone else what you have found out?**

Sod: The hidden. **What isn't said?**

'The use of Pardes can help learners to engage with traditional texts from whatever source – it's a wonderful tool to use in order to engage with scriptural reasoning and can be applied to an enormous range of activities and situations.

But most of all it is a spiritual tool – opening up vistas and hidden depths, stimulating curiosity, engaging with the imagination and enabling creativity – that spark of the Almighty that is within us all!'

Laurie Rosenberg

What is PARDES?

Pardes is made up of the initial letter of four Hebrew words.

In Hebrew the acronym PRDS makes the word Pardes which means 'paradise', literally an orchard.

To read is to explore paradise or to pick fruits in a heavenly orchard!

In this section Laurie helps you **engage in Pardes with your children,** applying the principles underpinning Pardes:

- delving deeper into a story from the Torah – the First Five Books of the Hebrew Bible;
- unpicking a school rule or two; and
- giving children the confidence to become more engaged with the Bible, and other texts they encounter, both sacred and secular, as they move through school.

RE Today weblink:

www.retoday.org.uk

For additional materials – including a worked example of teaching the story of Abraham and Isaac using this approach – go to the termly curriculum materials download section of the RE Today website: www.retoday.org.uk.

See also

Teachers TV: Using Stories the Jewish Way http://www.teachers.tv/

The Living Torah (English edition), a new translation based on traditional Jewish sources, is excellent as a reference for teachers. It is available from Amazon for about £12.00.

Use this PaRDeS template in order to help learners to unpack text

Title of story:

P'shat
The literal – what is being said?

Remez
Hint – interpretation – what does the text mean?

D'rash
How would you tell someone else – story or drama?

Sod
The hidden – what needn't be stated?

A PaRDeS approach to unpacking the Ten Commandments!

For the teacher

The Ten Commandments are found in Exodus, Chapter 20, and verses 1-14. From these deceptively simple statements the entire legal system of the Judeo-Christian world evolved.

Using a Jewish approach to story and text, each of the Ten Commandments can be taken apart and examined through the prism of Pardes to reveal an enormous amount of depth. Learners can apply the principles of the Ten Commandments through their own life experiences.

Let's look at the Second Commandment. At a literal level it says that no carved image can be made, but the meaning is much deeper since it could also refer to not idolising material possessions. This could start a wonderful **discussion** on materialism, celebrity, the media. At another level the children could **make up a play** about the danger of wanting 'more and more' – just think of those playground spats over football cards!

The only commandment to include a reward is reserved for those who honour their parents; a good family life is a healthy life – and thus the reward is implicit.

I I am the Lord your God who brought you out of the land of Egypt.

II You shall not make for yourself any idols.

III You shall not take the name of God in vain.

IV Remember the Sabbath day, to keep it holy. Six days you do all your work, but on the Sabbath you shall not work nor your family, your workers, your cattle and the stranger in your midst.

V Honour your father and your mother, so that your days may be long upon the land.

VI You shall not murder.

VII You shall not commit adultery.

VIII You shall not steal.

IX You shall not lie about your neighbour.

X You shall not be jealous of your neighbour's house - nor anything that is your neighbour's.

Suggested activities for the learners

- Choose any one of the Commandments. Use the **Pardes template** to delve into the real meaning behind the literal translation. Use **drama and story, art and cartoons** and always try to make a reference to today – even though the Ten Commandments were written over 3000 years ago!

- The line drawing above shows a section of a stained glass window from a synagogue. – The Ten Commandments are represented by key words. Ask pupils to design their **own stained glass window**, and come up with a key word to represent each of the Commandments.

A worked example using the Eighth Commandment: 'You shall not steal'

- Ask children to tell you what they think this Commandment means. At a literal level (**P'shat**) this simply means never take anything that doesn't belong to you.

- At a deeper level (**Remez**) the law becomes more fuzzy; for instance, what about if you found a knife, a weapon, illegal drugs – and these were confiscated, or simply taken without 'consent'? This 'stealth' could be considered as saving another life! Judaism also talks about stealing another person's reputation – the notion of gossip. What has been uttered can never, ever be taken back – our spoken word is permanent!

- In pairs or small groups ask children to discuss these deeper ideas about 'stealing' and construct a drama (**D'rash**) to express one scenario.

- Finally, explore the hidden (**Sod**). These are the *consequences* of stealing.

And now for some fun!

For the teacher

The idea of this activity is produce a 'good news' newspaper – using the Ten Commandments as a guideline.

Children will work in groups, each having a range of newspapers, comics or magazines according to age, ability, interests and understanding.

By using the Ten Commandments – or a version of them – children will 'cut out' stories that break one of or any of the Commandments. Each group, for instance, could concentrate on a particular Commandment, and by using the principles underpinning Pardes, the relevance of the Ten Commandments can be brought up to date.

Find some punchy headlines e.g.:

Thieves Rob Pensioner

By locating headlines like this and cutting them out along with the associated story, children begin to learn what can remain in their 'newspaper' and what needs to be removed.

It's even possible for 'bad' stories and headlines to be displayed and reasons given for their removal.

Activities and outcomes

- Children can create a collage of newspaper stories that clearly break one or any of the Ten Commandments.

- If a group has worked on a single newspaper and removed stories, pictures and articles that transgress the Ten Commandments, then it is possible to 'cut and paste' the remaining stories and articles (if any!) into a 'good news' newspaper.

- Apply these principles to digital media. Older children may be able to take a two-minute news bulletin on the radio and digitally 'cut out' stories that they consider break the Ten Commandments.

- Sod: what isn't said is a real tool of the journalist and what a story leaves out is often as important as what is left in. Children may want to discuss this in terms of a moral to a story or perhaps how a moral could be built into a story.

Other applications

You might wish to try using Pardes on a variety of situations and settings.

The matrix below is based on the principles underpinning Pardes. Identify a text, story, picture, an idea – or even a point of dispute between two pupils (a form of arbitration) in the centre.

Pupils working individually, in pairs, or in groups fill in the tiles surrounding the centre of the matrix with the ideas being discussed.

The example below uses a school rule. I have simply set out some points for discussion!

So use Pardes and enjoy!

Use these spaces to make notes of the discussions

P'shat
The literal meaning, without any interpretation.

Remez
Interpretation! What is meant by running? Does the rule apply equally inside or outside? What if there's a fire?

No running in school

D'rash
Can the pupils think of a drama or a sketch to show what happens if the rule is broken?
What about a series of pictures or drawings to show what happens if you do run?

Sod
What are the consequences of running in school?

Use these spaces to make notes of the discussions

P'shat
The literal meaning, without any interpretation.

Remez
Interpretation!

Issue

D'rash
Think of a drama or a sketch to show.....

Sod
What isn't said?

Wisdom and story from the Bible for 9-11s: wisdom card game

For the teacher

- The Bible is like other sacred texts in that it provides for wisdom to develop in the reader's own mind and life.

- Bible study may appear to be a boring activity from the outsiders' viewpoint, but in Britain today Bible study in small groups is perhaps the biggest activity of adult education in the nation.

- The widely popular 'Alpha Course' uses biblical wisdom to explore all sorts of moral and spiritual questions. Around 200,000 people have participated in the United Kingdom, with many millions worldwide. In the UK, many hundreds of thousands of people read the Bible every day.

Introducing the activity

- This activity aims to enable pupils to engage with questions of meaning and value through exploring what the Bible says. It is set up here as a card game for four pupils to play in a group.

How to play the game

- From a deck of 36 cards, each pupil is dealt a hand of five. They play by picking up and discarding cards until they have a hand of five cards that they think are wise.

- All the cards carry a carefully chosen quotation from the Bible, so the game enables pupils to identify biblical wisdom that appeals to them.

- There are four varied suggestions for the use of the cards and for following up the game on page 26.

The value of this activity

RE does pretty well at introducing stories from the Bible to pupils, but getting children thinking about the Bible's wisdom teaching is found less often. This is a shame, because pupils of 9–11 years of age can develop insight and discernment skills through exploring biblical wisdom. This activity will get them started.

Expectations and outcomes

If pupils can say 'yes' to some of these, they are working at the level shown.

I can...

	I can...
2 I can...	• retell a story from the Bible • respond sensitively to the wisdom of the Bible for myself through talking and discussion.
3 I can...	• describe some of the things the Bible says are wise • make links between my ideas about what is wise, and ideas from the Bible.
4 I can...	• use the language of Bible study to show that I understand how and why Christians think the Bible is sacred • apply some ideas about wisdom to situations in my own life and the lives of others.
5 I can...	• explain similarities and differences between the wisdom of the Bible and other people's ideas • give my own views about mysterious questions on life's meanings and values, taking account of ideas from the Bible.

RE Today weblink:

www.retoday.org.uk

A PowerPoint to introduce this work to pupils is available for subscribers on the RE Today website (www.retoday.org.uk), together with a reference sheet for teachers that shows the source of each biblical quotation.

- Copy the next three pages onto card, and cut them to equal sizes, making enough sets for pupils to play in groups of four. It helps to do each set on different coloured card.
- Play the game by dealing five cards to each person. In turns, take a new one (unseen) and discard one. The aim is to collect a hand of five cards that are 'wise for you today'. Then do the activities from page 26.

Love your neighbour as much as you love yourself.	If you love money, then you can't love God as well.	Nothing outside will make you dirty. It's what is inside that can mess up your life.
Love does not get jealous, angry or rude.	Let your 'Yes' mean 'Yes' and your 'No' mean 'No'. Don't pile up empty words.	If someone takes your coat, then offer him your shirt as well. Give generously, then people will be generous to you too.
Don't worry about tomorrow – tomorrow will take care of itself.	Feed the hungry, care for the homeless, be kind to the desperate. That's what religion really means.	Work for six days in the week, but rest for one day out of seven.
You'll be happy if you are hungry and thirsty for justice. One day it will be yours!	Don't judge others and then they won't judge you.	People who are pure hearted are blessed. They will get to see God!

If you forgive others, then they will forgive you.	A generous person will prosper. If you refresh others, you'll be refreshed yourself.	Lazy hands make people poorer, but hardworking hands gain wealth.
Hate what is evil: hold on strongly to what is good.	**Do not be proud, but be friends with those whom others leave out.**	**Keep all filthy and unkind talk out of your mouth.**
If I know the future and if I give my money to the poor, that's all useless if I don't have love.	**Do not be overwhelmed by evil. Instead, overwhelm evil with goodness.**	Live your life like this: do what is just. Love what is merciful. Walk with God. Don't be proud.
Wisdom is more precious than rubies or jewels. Nothing else you want compares with wisdom.	One of the best things in life is when brothers and sisters live together in unity.	Beware of the tongue! Like a little rudder on a big ship it can turn you around. Speak carefully!

Be thankful whatever happens.	**Love rejoices in what is right.**	Don't worry about money and possessions – look at the flowers that do no work. No one else dresses as beautifully as them.
When troubles come – and they will – accept them as if they were from God.	Human beings look at the outside appearance, but God sees what really matters – your heart!	Get rid of lies and speak truthfully because we are all members of one body.
Good morals can be ruined by bad company.	Mickey-takers wind up a whole city, but wise people reduce anger.	When you do something generous, don't go on about it. God sees every secret act of kindness.
There's nothing better than a good friend who always takes care of you.	Be happy while you are young and enjoy yourself before you get old.	When you pray, don't babble away! God hears in secret, and will reward your secret prayer.

Following up the learning with speaking, listening and writing

In these four activities, teachers may wish to keep the focus on the Bible's teaching itself, but it may alternatively be good to use a wider range of 'wise sayings'. These might come from the children themselves, from families and other adults, from other religious traditions or from collections of quotations (there are plenty of these online if you search).

Activity 1 Why is it wise?

Ask pupils to move to a different group of four, taking their final hand of five wise cards with them. In turn, they are to share one of their cards and give a reason why it is wise, listening to others in the group as well.

Pupils might use these prompts:

- I've chosen this wise saying because…

- What I like about this one is…

- This will make life better by…

- My main reason for choosing this one is…

Activity 2 Application: what difference would this wisdom make?

Ask the pupils to create cartoons in two parts for a card of their choice. The first part of the cartoon shows what happens when people follow this wisdom. The second part shows what happens if people do the opposite of the wisdom on the card. Give pupils positive encouragement to make their 'not following wisdom' cartoons as wacky and wild as they choose.

RE Today weblink:

www.retoday.org.uk

There are support materials for these four activities on the RE Today website: www.retoday.org.uk.

Activity 3 Ranking 10 wise sayings with a partner

Ask pupils to take their five cards and five for their partner, and discuss in pairs if they can rank the wise sayings from 1 to 10, wisest at the top. Why is this difficult?

Then 'snowball' the pairs, getting into groups of four, to see what was the same and different about the ranked order. Focus the discussion on the varieties of wisdom and their application (a Level 4 skill in RE).

Activity 4 Creative expression: three examples of wisdom and images

Ask the pupils to choose their top three wisdom cards, and choose or create an illustration for each one. This can be done for a classroom display, or can be made into a class book, with a page from each child. Collecting images from internet sources, collaging from magazines or drawing and painting are all good ways to express the 'image of wisdom'.

Exploring perspectives on biblical story: a mind game

For the teacher

- This activity is flexible and imaginative, and enables children to develop their creative skills.

- It connects well with aspects of literacy learning for Year 5 and Year 6 (9–11s).

- It does not assume knowledge of all the biblical stories referred to – but good RE might cover many of them.

Speculation is a thinking skill that RE needs more

It provides for creative and imaginative work for pupils of many different abilities, and is fun.

- Use the statements below as starters for paired group talk and/or written response.

- Link the activity to the 'wisdom learning' on the preceding pages by asking pupils to think what wise advice they could give to Eve, Noah, the Princess, Moses, Joshua, Jonah and others.

Let's speculate.

What would it be like, how would it feel, what would you think, say, or pray if you were...

- at the gate of the Garden of Eden when Adam and Eve were thrown out.

- outside the ark, speaking to Noah who is inside.

- in love with someone in the Egyptian army, drowned after the nasty business at the Red Sea.

- outside the walls of Jericho when Joshua sounded the call for the brass section to strike up.

- in front of the burning bush with Moses.

- on the banks of the Nile with the Egyptian princess when the original Moses basket floated past.

- in the temple when 12-year-old Jesus went to town on the questions for the chief priests and elders.

- at the stable with the shepherds.

- up the tree with Zacchaeus.

- round the fire at the trial of Jesus with Peter when he denied Jesus.

- with the women friends of Jesus at the empty tomb.

- in the barracks when the soldiers guarding the tomb tried to excuse themselves after the stone rolled away.

- a companion of Saul as he fell to the ground outside Damascus.

- in the whale with Jonah.

What matters more than money? Reflecting on values using a traditional story and a story from another culture

For the teacher

The following lesson activities use two stories to help pupils in the 8–10 age range to think for themselves about the importance of money, and about values.

Using religious and cultural story to explore issues about money and wealth is particularly appropriate at a time when it is hard to escape from the view that cash value matters most. All religions bear witness to values beyond money and wealth, as do non-religious ethical life stances like Humanism.

Cross-curricular links

The following four pages make particular links to **literacy**. In England, the literacy strategy provides for pupils at Year 4 and Year 5 to develop their skills with reference to **narratives such as traditional stories and stories from other cultures**.

This unit uses a story of Jesus from first-century Palestine and a traditional Asian story to provoke thinking about values and wealth.

The activities use a repeating skill development pattern to enable pupils to use images and texts reflectively and creatively.

The approach places a story or picture at the centre of a series of questions or sentence starters to structure pupil's paired or group talk. Page 29 features a story from another culture. Pages 30 and 31 offer two ways of enabling pupils to respond to the story of Jesus about the rich man – one in text and one using the Vie de JesusMafa artwork from Africa. Page 32 uses an image of banknotes to structure pupils, own reflections on the issues raised in the two stories.

RE Today weblink:

www.retoday.org.uk

Subscribers can download pages 29-32 for use in the classroom from the RE Today website www.retoday.org.uk (go to REtoday Curriculum Books web supplement).

Ask pupils to complete the speech bubbles and after 15 minutes ask them to read out their responses and compare their own answers to those of others.

Expectations and outcomes

If pupils can say 'yes' to some of these, they are working at the level shown.

I can...

2 I can...	• retell a story about wealth and poverty • respond sensitively to the meaning of a story about wealth and poverty for myself.
3 I can...	• describe the teaching about wealth that is contained in a story • make a link between the story and an attitude to wealth today • make a link from the stories to my own attitudes to money and to poverty.
4 I can...	• use the right words to describe why these stories have been told for hundreds of years • show my understanding of the ways these two stories are similar and different • apply ideas about wealth, generosity or community for myself by telling/writing a story of my own.

1. What matters most to the fisherman in the story?

2. Give five words that sum up what you think the rich businesswoman is like.

3. What are the differences between the rich businesswoman and the fisherman?

A story from another culture:
The fisherman and the rich businesswoman

One day a rich businesswoman was on holiday walking along the seashore when she met a fisherman. The businesswoman was horrified to find the fisherman lying down having a rest beside his boat.

'Why aren't you out fishing?' she asked.

'I've already caught enough fish for today,' he said.

So the rich businesswoman asked the fisherman why he didn't catch more than he needed.

'What would I do with more fish?' he asked.

'Well, you could sell the fish that you don't need to eat, and then you would make some money. Then you could save up more and more money so you could get a motor fixed to your boat, so you could go into deeper waters to catch more fish. Then you could sell the fish and use the money to buy better nets so you could catch more fish. Then you could sell that fish and buy another boat with the money you make. One day you might even have a lot of boats. Then you would be rich like I am.'

'What would I do when I am rich?' he asked.

'When you're rich you could sit down, take it easy, relax and enjoy life,' the businesswoman said.

'But I'm doing that right now,' said the fisherman.

Story from Asia, source unknown.

4. What do you think of the two different attitudes to work in the story?

5. Who would you rather be in this story?

Why?

6. What is the message of this story in your opinion?

1. What mattered most to this farmer?

   How can you tell?

2. Think of four other things that the farmer could have done when his crops did so well.

3. In the story, the farmer does not reply to God. What do you think he would say?

A story from the Bible: Jesus' Parable of the Rich Fool

Jesus told this story:

One year, the richest man in town had a great big load of bumper crops. Everything grew twice as well as expected. He said to himself, 'What can I do? I don't have a place large enough to store everything.' Later, he said, 'I know what I'll do. I'll tear down my barns and build bigger ones, where I can store all my grain and other goods. Then I'll say to myself, "You have stored up enough good things to last for years to come. Live it up! Eat, drink, and enjoy yourself."' But God said to him, 'You fool! Tonight you will die. Then who will get what you have stored up?'

Jesus said: 'This is what happens to people who store up everything for themselves, but are poor in the sight of God.'

Bible, Luke 12:16-21

4. What was Jesus trying to teach people in this parable?

5. How much do you think money and possessions matter in life?

   What things matter more than money?

6. What are your own attitudes to money?

   Why?

7. I'm not sure about...

6. I observed

5. It's obvious that...

4. I can see...

3. My title for the picture would be...

because

8. I want to ask about...

9. An opinion of mine is...

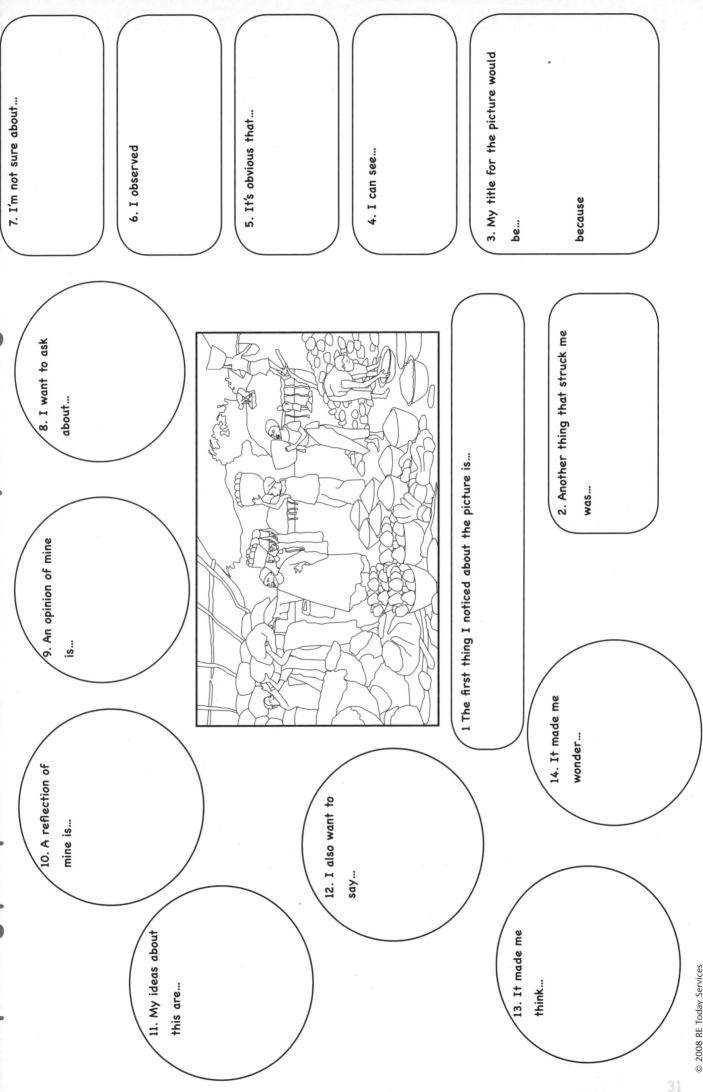

1 The first thing I noticed about the picture is...

2. Another thing that struck me was...

10. A reflection of mine is...

11. My ideas about this are...

12. I also want to say...

13. It made me think...

14. It made me wonder...

Money, Money, Money

1. The first thing that struck me looking at this was...

6. My deepest thoughts about this work are...

2. This picture makes me imagine...

5. My questions about money are...

3. I think the message of this picture for me is...

4. Some people think being generous is more important than having money. I think.